THEY GLORIFIED MARY... WE GLORIFIED RICE

A Catholic-Lutheran Lexicon

by
Janet Letnes Martin and Suzann (Johnson) Nelson
Caragana Press
Box 396
Hastings, MN 55033

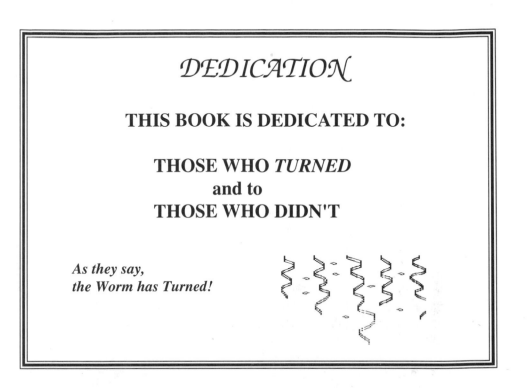

DEDICATION

THIS BOOK IS DEDICATED TO:

THOSE WHO *TURNED*
and to
THOSE WHO DIDN'T

*As they say,
the Worm has Turned!*

TABLE of CONTENTS

AN EPISTLE TO OUR READERS

Dear Catholic and Lutheran Friends:

- *You who have remained true to your faith and believe in your heart you're right;*
- *You who have turned, thus upsetting all the relatives;*
- *You who never knew there was a difference and still don't because you're a Christmas-Easter attender, but now that you're a little older, you're getting curious; and*
- *You who never gave it any thought!*

It was while we were taking a coffee break from writing our best-selling book, **Cream Peas on Toast**, that it dawned on us that the world needed us to write a few little books comparing and contrasting such things as Lutheran and Catholic ways, Town and Country ways, and all the baggage and trappings that go with these kinds of things. (*Why nobody had ever thought of this idea, we'll never know*).

Well, before we had drained the pot, we had drafted our Town and Country Lexicon aptly named, **They Had Stores and We Had Chores**. (*One of Janet's neighbors who grew up Out East and knew city things through and through, came up with the title*).

Growing up in rural areas on farms, both of us knew we wore kerchiefs and overshoes while our cousins from the suburbs had *floosified* the language and called them scarves and Kickerinos, repectively. But now, even though we both live in town and know some town talk too, we're still more comfortable with the country vernacular. We still prefer to call our Brillo pads "chore boys" and our accelerators "foot-feeds". (*You can take the girl out of the country, but why bother trying to take the country out of the girl? We'll never know).*

This Catholic and Lutheran Lexicon was more difficult to write than the Town and Country Lexicon was — at least half of it. You see, both of us were baptized into the Lutheran faith *(November '46)*, and grew up attending Sunday School at different Our Saviour's Lutherans. *(In '57, Janet had perfect attendance but Suzann didn't — she was down with the Asiatic Flu for a week even though there weren't any Orientals living in her area, but there had been a visiting missionary from Formosa who came to give a chalk-talk and could have left the flu bug, too).*

Both of us went to Lutheran Bible Camps, faithfully attended Luther League and Luther League Conventions, graduated from Augsburg (Lutheran) College, and repeated all of **Luther's Small Catechism** for our pastors *(all five parts in 15 minutes without taking a breath – in May '61 – kind of like this* *sentence).* You could say we were dripping wet with Lutheran heritage from the time we were born until, (*and it goes without saying*), we both married good Scandinavian-Lutheran boys from rural areas. ***This is most certainly true!***

Well, now you know why we had a tough time writing half of this book – the Catholic half. That is why we came up with something that might seem part theology and part mythology.

Since Lutherans don't know much about patron saints, novenas, living rosaries, ejaculations (*uffda*), or St. Anthony's ability to find things as quick as a Mom could, we had to do some digging. We could have used the Patron Saint of Hopeless Causes like the Catholics have but, at that time, we didn't know his or her name, so we did what we were taught to do. We used our heads and figured things out for ourselves.

We read the **Baltimore Catechism** to see how different it really was from Luther's. (*It was different. Who's a person supposed to believe nowadays, anyway?*). We also skimmed missals and books written on Catholicism by authors who were serious about academia and by those who were just trying to make a quick buck by poking fun of paraochial school nuns.

In our research, we met with kids from Creighton University who said we needed *to turn* Catholic, and that everything we needed to know we could find in Maccabees. (*We found a copy and read it, but we couldn't figure out what we needed to know*). We also asked intimate questions of our dear Catholic friends — questions such as:

- •What does it feel like to dance?
- •Does it get hot in a confessional booth?
- •Does your face turn red if you aren't telling the whole truth?

- If the guy in front of you is in there too long, do you feel kind of smug and think that he's got a mortal on his chest, and you're just standing in line to report on a couple of venials?
- Did you ever sneak a Sloppy Joe on Friday?
- Can you really see your underpants in your patent leather shoes, or did the nuns just make that up?
- Did the netting that the nuns shoved down the front of your prom dress (*because the low neck was too risque*) itch as bad as the long brown wool-connected-to-a-garter-belt stockings did?
- Do you have to pay cold cash to get out of purgatory or can you just light some candles?
- Did you really pray for us poor lost Lutheran souls as much as you said you did?

•Did the relics in the altar look like old dry bones just like in the song?

We want to thank our good Catholic friends for answering our puzzling questions. Some of these friends have read the draft of this book and have laughed with approval. Our intent is not to be irreverent. If anyone is offended by anything we wrote, we apologize.

If you like this book but think we missed some important comparisons and contrasts, send us your ideas. Who knows — if we get enough material, we'll write Volume II. If we use your idea, you'll get a free book. Why, you can't beat that, then!

Beste hilsner,

Janet   *Suzann*

Chapter I
PECKING ORDERS:

Catholic Orders, Synod Stuff and Mary

They had the Pope...
  We had Martin Luther.

They had the Holy Roman Emporer...
  We had Hans Nielsen Hauge.

They had Cardinals...
  We had delegates.

They had Archbishops...
    We had synod presidents.

They had Monsignors...
    We had bishops' brown-nosers.

They had Vicars...
    We had Vicks inhalers.

They had Fathers...
We had reverends.

They had Priests...
We had pastors.

They had Brothers...
We had brethren.

They had renegade, separated Brethren...
   We had separated brethren who *they* called
   Protestants.

They had Friars...
   We had fryers too, and pullets.

They had Monks in Monasteries...
   We had Norwegian bachelors on farms.
   (Herman's Hermits; Herman, MN.)

They had Fulton Sheen and Archbishop Roach...
> We had Reuben Youngdahl and
> Bernt C. Opsal.

They have Andrew Greeley from Chicago...
> We have Martin Marty from Chicago.
> (We also have his son, John – the Lutheran
>   politician in St. Paul – who ran against
>   Governor Arne Carlson, Swedish-American.)

They had Catharine of Avignon...
> We had "Kitty, My Rib".

They had Mother Superior...
    We had Superior / Highly Superior ratings
    at band contests.

They had Mother Superior...
    We had Lake Superior.

They had Nuns...
    We had flustered Sunday
    School superintendents.

They had some mean Nuns...
    We had some mean streaks.

They had Novices...
    We went with the Tried and True.

They sent Missionaries and Things to Mexico...
    We sent Missionaries and Stuff to
    Madagascar.

They had Princess Grace of Monaco...

We had Princess Kay of the Milky Way.

They had Holy Mothers...
We had hefty Mothers.

They had ladies of Perpetual Help...
  We had ladies of perpetual motion.

They had Brothers and Sisters and Fathers and Mothers Superior...
  We had brothers and sisters and dads and hefty moms.

They had Godparents...
  We had sponsors.

They had Chanters...
   We had *Klokkars.*

They had Altar Boys...
   We had naughty boys who couldn't sit still,
   and who couldn't memorize as well as the
   girls.

They had German-Catholics...
   We had German-Lutherans.

They had Vatican Councils...
We had *The Diet of Worms.*

They followed Vatican II...
We followed the various Lutheran splits and mergers.

They had Archdiocese...
We had headquarters.

They had Diocese...
    We had synods.

They had a Council of Catholics...
    We had church councils.

They had Orders...
    We took orders.

MARY:

They glorified Mary...
We glorified rice.

They pictured Mary with a Halo...
    We pictured her by the manger.

They had the Holy Mary...
    We had the human Mary.

They had the Virgin Mary...
    We had the she-pondered-all-these-
    things-in-her-heart Mary.

*They said, "Benedicta tu in mulieribus,
et benedictus fructus ventris tui Jesus"...**

We said, "*Velsignet er de saktmodige;
Velsignet er ydmyke mennesker*". **

. . . .

*Blessed art thou among women, and blessed is the
fruit of thy womb, Jesus.

**Blessed are the meek; Blessed are the poor in spirit.

They had Anna, the Mother of Mary...
We had Anna — the lady next door —
who made really good *sandbakkler*.

Chapter II
HOW FIRM A
FOUNDATION:

Buildings and Grounds,
Services and Stuff

They call it the Holy Catholic Church...
We call it the Holy Christian Church.

They believe the church is a Mighty Fortress...
We believe *A Mighty Fortress Is Our God.*

They had cathedrals...
We had *stav* churches.

They had spires...
   We had steeples.

They named it St. Peter...
   We named it St. Paul.

They had the Basilica of St. Paul...
   We had *Mindekirken*.

They belonged to parishes...
> We belonged to congregations.

They had parish halls...
> We had church basements.

They had Catholic parochial schools...
> We had consolidated public schools.

They had rectories...
     We had parsonages.

They ate in the refectory...
     We ate in fellowship halls and in
     church basements.

They had vaults...
     We had faults.

They buried Saints and Popes in church walls and under the floor...

We buried
ministers
and Martin
in the ground
with everyone
else.

They had sextons who took care of their buildings...

    We had janitors, and nothing to do with sex.

They had Latin Services...

    We had Norwegian Services.

They had High Mass...

    We had high noon.

They went to mass...
We went to 9 o'clock services.

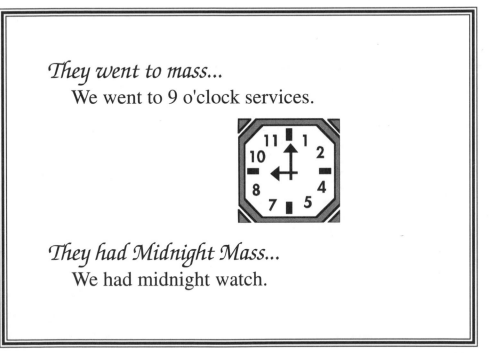

They had Midnight Mass...
We had midnight watch.

They listened to homilies...
  We sat through sermons.

They had confession booths...
  We had Sunday School dividers.

They had Holy Water...
  We had well water.

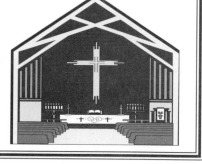

They had kneeling rails...
We had hymnal racks.

They had crucifixes...
We had crosses.

*They had silk paraments
on the altar...*
We had *Hardangersøm.*

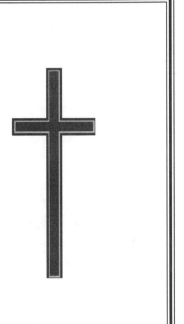

They stored relics in the altar...
    We stored them in the storeroom.

They decorated with statues and relics...
    We decorated with flags and banners.

They decorated
with holly and ivy...

        We decorated with
        hollyhocks and glads.

Chapter III
WHEN THE SAINTS GO MARCHING IN

They had Patron Saints...
  We basically fended for ourselves.

They had special Saints...
  We had the Sainthood of all Believers.

They had All Saints' Day...
  We had Reformation Sunday.

They had designated martyrs...
    We thought we all were.

They had Anne, the Patron Saint of House-wives...
    We had County Extension Agents.

They had a Patron Saint for Pawnbrokers...
    We paid cash so we could be *skuldfri*.

They had Martha, the Patron Saint for Cooks...
> We had Betty Crocker.

They had Theresa of Avila...
> We had Rebecca of Sunnybrook.

They counted on St. Jude for Good Luck...
> We dried wishbones on the
> window sill over the kitchen sink.

They had Saint Christopher statues for guidance in the car...

We had **NESW** balls for guidance in the car.

They had St. Francis of Assisi who blessed animals...

We had 4H Project Leaders and curry combs.

They had Joan of Arc...
We had Ruth (Mrs. The Reverend Billy) Graham.

They had Saints, Timothy and Titus, to work against stomach disorders...
We had hot water bottles and Tums.

They called on St. Herbert in times of drought...
We prayed for rain directly.

They called upon Teresa of Avila to relieve headaches...

    We took two aspirin and kept pluggin' away.

They had Mother Theresa...

    We had Marie Sandvig.

They revered St. Patrick...

    We revered St. Olaf.

They had Martin De Porres,
Patron Saint of Hairdressers...

We had Richard Hudnut.

*TONY, TONY,
LOOK AROUND.*

*SOMETHING'S LOST
and
MUST BE FOUND!*

GUDMUND, GUDMUND,
USE YOUR HEAD.

IT'S UNDER THE DRESSER
or
UNDER THE BED!

They counted on St. Anthony to find things...
  We counted on our mothers.

They knew St. Anthony could help find things...
  We knew things were probably where we
  put them in the first place.

They believed St. Anthony would help find things...
  We believed stuff would turn up sooner
  or later.

Chapter IV

BEHAVIORS and BELIEFS

They went to church on Saturday...
   We went to church on Sunday.

They took vows of chastity, poverty and obedience...
   We didn't have to.

They believe in the infallibility of the Pope...
   We believe everyone has a few bad days
   now and then.

They had Holy Days of Obligation...
    We had chores every day.

They made Novenas...
    We had neighborhood prayer chains.

They had Stations of the Cross...
    We had the Old Rugged.

They believed all had sinned, except Mary...
We believed all had sinned and fallen short.

They said, "Hail, Mary Full of Grace"...
We said, "What Does this Mean?"

They said, "Blessed are you among Women"...
We said, "How is This Done?"

They patronized and canonized...
   We simonized and sanitized.

They saved pagan babies...
   We saved heathens.

They had Saint Peter waiting at the gate...
   We had cows waiting at the gate.

They signed their kids over to the church...
    We signed the kids up for *VBS*.

They sometimes relaxed church law through dispensations...
    We made no exceptions.

They had alms for the poor...
    We had food baskets for the shut-ins.

They had immediate baptism...
   We had baptism when the relatives could
   make it.

They had eight to thirteen kids...
   We had two to seven.

They had seven Sacraments...
   We had two.

THEY THOUGHT THEY HAD THE TRUTH...

WE THOUGHT WE HAD THE TRUTH.

THEY THOUGHT WE WERE GOING TO HELL...

WE THOUGHT THEY WERE GOING TO HELL.

They had purgatory and limbo...
    We had limited choices.

They say the Rosary...
    We say, "Now I Lay Me."

They worried about backsliding...
    We worried about backbiting.

They burned incense...
    We burned the church mortgage papers.

They confessed to the Father...
　　We told Mom it was an accident.

They confessed all...
　　We got by with what we could.

They told all to the Priest...
　　We kept it all to ourselves.

They had incense...
　　We had Air Wick.

They say the Blessing before eating...
We say Grace.

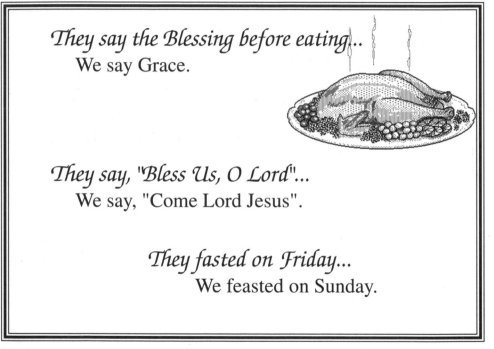

They say, "Bless Us, O Lord"...
We say, "Come Lord Jesus".

They fasted on Friday...
We feasted on Sunday.

They have the Petrine theology...
    We have the Pauline theology.

They memorized the Baltimore Catechism...
    We memorized **Luther's Small Catechism.**

They read Maccabees...
    We read anything put out by Augsburg
    Publishing House.

                    They read missals...
                        We read tracts.

They passed Baskets...
   We passed collection plates and
   kidney stones.

They chanted...
   We could read music.

They got Holy cards for memorization...
   We got gold, blue or red stars for
   "learning it by heart".

They slid in two minutes before Mass,
slid out right afterwards,
piled into their station wagons, and
went right home...

We arrived twenty minutes early
to get our regular pews and
stuck around afterwards for
coffee and bars.

They crossed themselves...
    We crossed our arms.

They genuflected...
    We sat still.

They knelt...
    We sat up straight.

They pointed their hands skyward...
    We folded our hands.

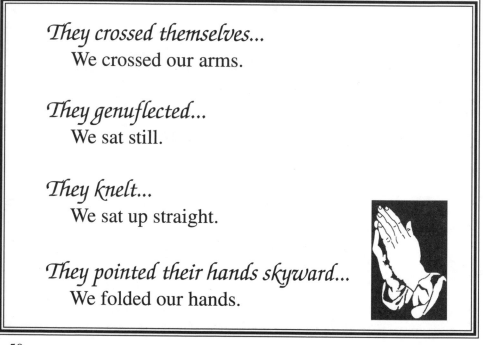

They put ash on their foreheads...
> We put ash in a tub to make soap for the Missions.

They believed in the Immaculate Conception...
> We believed in immaculate housekeeping.

They celebrated the Eucharist...
> We *took* Holy Communion, and celebrated anniversaries.

They lit candles...

We lit kerosene lamps.

They cut the Lord's Prayer short...
We finished it.

Chapter V

VISIONS
and
MYSTERIES

They saw visions...
   We saw things in black and white.

They saw visions...
   We saw things as they really were.

They had guardian angels...
   We didn't give them much thought.

They had weeping Madonnas...
We had sweaty kitchen workers.

They had crosses that turned to gold...
We had crosses that tarnished.

They had the Shroud of Turin...

We had old bathrobes for wisemen,
old sheets for Mary and Joseph,
gunny sacks with rope belts for shepherds
in the Christmas play, and
other miscellaneous swaddling clothes.

They had auras...
    We had flashlights.

They had mystics...
    We had Bible Camp experiences.

They looked for the Holy Grail...
    We looked for the Holy Ghost.

They had Blarney Stones...
    We had kidney stones.

They had shamrocks
for good luck...
    We had lucky rabbits feet.

They had the Blarney Stone...
    We had the Viking Runestone.

They had miracles...
    We had Miracle Whip.

They knew angels...
    We knew of them.

Chapter VI

SINS and INDULGENCES

They had plenary indulgences...
   We had plenty times we wanted to indulge.

They had venial and mortal sins...
   We had a-sin-is-a-sin sins.

They said, "Go and sin no more"...
   We had Norwegian-Lutheran guilt for life.

They danced...
   Dancing was a sin.

They went to town Saturday night for dances...

We went to town Saturday night for drawings.

They drank on Saturday nights...

We took baths on Saturday nights.

They danced...

We didn't dare.

They had wedding dances...
    We had wedding receptions.

They got annulments...
    We believed a rose by any other name
    was still a rose.

They danced...
    We couldn't risk
    getting that close.

They played bingo...
    We played hide and seek.

They played with face cards...
    We played with Rook cards.

They danced...
    We played musical chairs.

They had Whoopee John...
    We had whooping cough.

They had quilt raffles...
    We had cake walks.

They danced...
    We twirled around
    church basement poles.

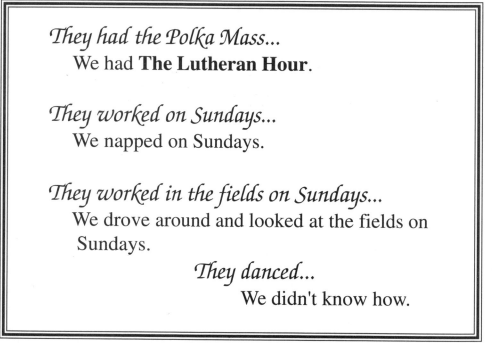

They had the Polka Mass...
    We had **The Lutheran Hour**.

They worked on Sundays...
    We napped on Sundays.

They worked in the fields on Sundays...
    We drove around and looked at the fields on
    Sundays.

            They danced...
                We didn't know how.

They were quick-tempered...
   We were slow to anger,
   but abounding in steadfast love.

They let it all out...
   We festered.

They danced...
   We couldn't reconcile dancing with
   leading a chaste and pure life.

They drank beer...
    We drank coffee.

They drank ale...
    We drank *Akevit*
    (but only in Norway).

They danced...
    We walked through the
    Valley of the Shadow of Death.

They served whiskey and rye drinks...

We served *Wasa* and rye breads.

They had Canadian whiskey...
We had Canadian thistle.

They danced...
We said, "*Fa'n Sjøl!*"

They had Father Flanagan's Boys' Home...
We had the Red Wing Reformatory.

They had the Legion of Decency...
We had hefty mothers
who stood their ground.

*They had Audrey Hepburn and
Julie Andrews...*
  We had Liv Ullman and the Andrew
  Sisters.

MOVIES

They had Annette Funicellio...
  We had Ingrid Bergman.

They sold indulgences...
　　We sold church anniversary cookbooks
　　and centennial plates.

They had indulgences...
　　We had common sense and moderation.

Chapter VII

FISHES and LOAVES and CHURCH PICNICS

They had a diet of fish...
  We had *The Diet of Worms.*

They ate tuna...
  We ate *torsk.*

They had fish frys...
  We had *lutefisk* suppers.

They ate Mrs. Paul's fishsticks...
We ate King Oscar's fishballs.

They fasted on Friday...
We feasted on Sunday.

They had Feast Days...
We had potluck suppers.

They ate Irish soda bread...
    We ate Scandinavian *flatbrød*.

They had scones...
    We had *krumkaker*.

They had Shrove Tuesday buns...
    We had *Sankta Lucia* buns.

They had Bailey's Irish Cream...
> We had creamery cream.

They had Irish Mulligan Stew...
> We had vegetable soup
> with dumplings and pearl barley.

They had cornbeef and cabbage for St. Patrick's Day...
> We had round steak and rutabagas for "ever-day".

They had tortillas...
    We had *lefse*.

They had Spanish olives...
    We had pickled
    pigs feet.

They cracked a beer...
    We cracked hazelnuts.

They had beef jerky...
We had dried beef.

They ate pasta...
We ate potatoes.

They had beanfeeds...
We had harvest festivals.

They ate Italian meatballs...
We ate Swedish meatballs.

They had fettuccine alfredo...
We had creamed new potatoes.

They had linguine...
We had leftovers.

They had chicken cacciatore...

We stirred together cut up chicken leftovers, cooked egg noodles, peas, cream of mushroom soup and salt in a *Hotdish* and added milk as a thinning agent for a meal with *real* flair.

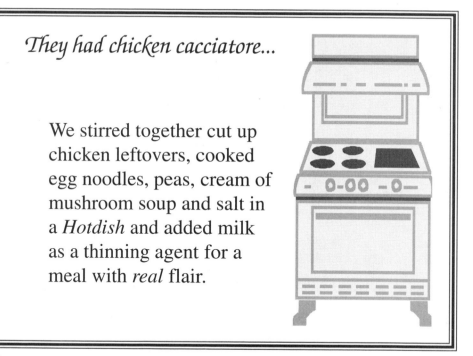

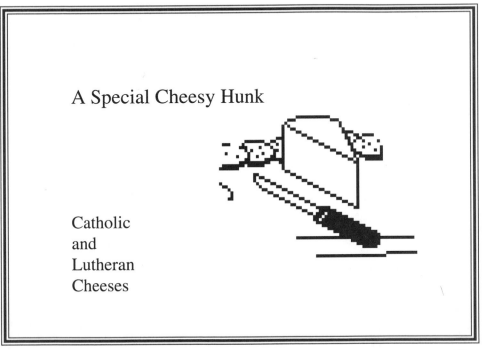

A Special Cheesy Hunk

Catholic
and
Lutheran
Cheeses

They had Camembert cheese...
    We had head cheese.

They had Ricotta cheese...
    We had cottage cheese.

They had Fontina cheese...
    We had *Jarlsberg*.

They had Mozzarella cheese...
    We had Velveeta cheese.

They had Roquefort cheese...
   We had *gammelost*.

They had Provolone cheese...
   We had *geitost*.

They had Romano cheese...
   We had *nøkkelost*.

They had cream cheese...
   We had Cheese Whiz!

For picnics, they had beer, brats, beans, coleslaw and watermelon;
their men played poker, and their women watched their twelve kids so they didn't run around like a bunch of heathens...

For picnics, we had glorified rice, scalloped potatoes and ham, pork and beans, red Jell-O with a
banana in it, buttered buns (light and dark), sweet,
dill, beet, watermelon and 7-day pickles, corn
relish, Watkins orange nectar and coffee with cream
and sugar lumps, Dixie Cups for the kids and three
kinds of cake (Devil's food, Angel food and marble or
— if you weren't too busy the day before the picnic —
you made white cake with 7-minute frosting and coconut
on top if you felt like it). After second and third help-
ings, our men took a snooze while our women
picked up, and then our men played horseshoes and
our women visited while our kids ran around like a
bunch of wild heathens on the loose.

GLORIFIED RICE

1 Box of Lemon Jell-O
1 Cup Boiling Water
1 Cup or less of Crushed Pineapple
2 Cups Boiled Rice (dry)
1 Cup Cream
4 Tablespoons Sugar
Salt to taste, unless worried about high blood pressure

Dissolve Jell-O in boiling water. When cool & thick, whip it to the consistency of heavy cream. Add the rice, pine- apple, whipped cream and salt – if you use it.

Pour into any desired mold to set. When set, unmold on serving plate. Garnish with whipped cream & a red cherry on top.

Makes about 10 servings or so, depending.

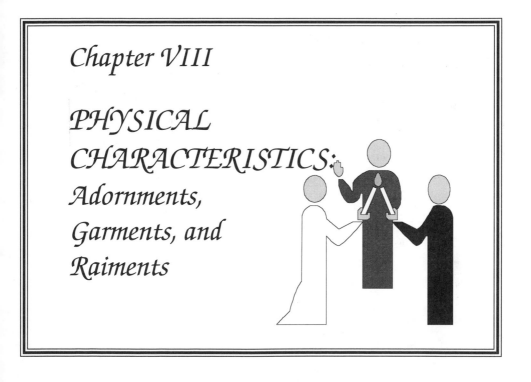

Chapter VIII

PHYSICAL CHARACTERISTICS:
Adornments,
Garments, and
Raiments

They had dark hair...
We had light hair.

They had brown eyes...
We had blue eyes.

They were average...
We had strong backs
and thick extremities.

They were olive-skinned...
   We were fair-skinned.

They tanned...
   We burned.

They wore habits...
   We had them.

They wore a lot of Irish tweed...
   We wore a lot of stuff made from flour
   sacks.

They went to church as is...

We dressed up in our
Sunday church clothes.

They wore AA shoes and EE bras...
We wore EE shoes and AA bras.

They wore draped mantillas...
    We wore knotted kerchiefs and crocheted
    shawls.

They wore lacy veils...
    We wore beaded hairnets.

They wore hats every Sunday...
                    We wore hats on
                    Easter if we were lucky.

They had skull caps...
We had cradle cap.

They had Cardinals who wore red hats for investiture...
We wore red hats
for deer hunting.

Their Priests wore robes and funny collars...
Our Pastors did too, but they didn't look
Catholic. (But our Free'ers just wore suits).

They had white First Communion dresses...
  We had white wedding dresses.

They wore any color dress for Confirmation
(as long as it had some red on it)...
  We wore white Confirmation dresses.

They got Confirmation names...
  We got Confirmation watches.

They wore plaid, pleated jumpers...
We wore small-print, gathered skirts,
(with side-zippers, of course).

They wore pointed collars...
We wore Peter Pan collars.

They wore patent leather shoes...
We wore buckle-up shoes.

They used a lot of make-up...
    We dabbed a little loose powder
    here and there now and then.

They used lipstick...
    We used chapstick.

They wore dangly earrings or showy clip-ons...
    We didn't poke holes in our bodies (which were
    the Lord's temples), and the clip-ons itched.

They wore clear polish on their nails to school...
>   We used it to stop runs in our nylons.

They wore colored polish on their nails...
>   We used it to mark initials on our cakepans.

They wore colored nail polish on their toes...
>   We clipped them straight across like the
>   doctor told us to.

They wore St. Christopher medals...
We wore *I am a Lutheran* pins.

They wore Mary Medallions...
We wore *sølje* pins.

They wore crosses on chains,
(the bigger the better)...

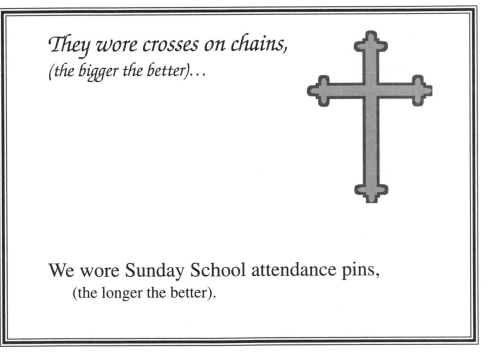

We wore Sunday School attendance pins,
  (the longer the better).

They had clandestine rings...
  We had mood rings.

Their mother rings were in a cluster...
  Ours were in one short row.

They carried rosaries...
  We carried nickels tied in the corner of a
  hanky.

Chapter IX

*CULTURE and
HIGH BROW STUFF:*

Music, Art and Literature

They revered relics and saints...
We revered church anniversary plates and
Bing and Grøndahl Christmas plates.

They had relics...
We had hand-me-downs.

They had three classes of relics...
We didn't throw things out either.

They had a May queen...
We had *Sankta Lucia.*

They made spiritual bouquets...
We picked lilac bouquets.

They had Lilies of the Field...
We picked mustard in the field.

They had Whitsunday...
We had Pentecost.

They had Pentecost...
We had Ascension.

They had First Communion...
We had catechization.

They had altar, Holy, and bingo cards...
    We had Get Well, Anniversary, and
    Sympathy cards.

*They kept their Lenten donations
in mite boxes...*
    We kept ours in
    slotted dime folders.

They had Catholic Charities...
  We had *Lutheran World Relief.*

They had the Archbishop's Appeal...
  We had the Concordia College
  C-400 Club .

They gave money to pagan babies...
  We gave money to orphanages.

They went to "CCD"...
    We went to Released Time.

*They got insurance from the Independent
Order of Foresters and from Catholic Aid...*
    We got insurance from AAL and
    Lutheran Brotherhood.

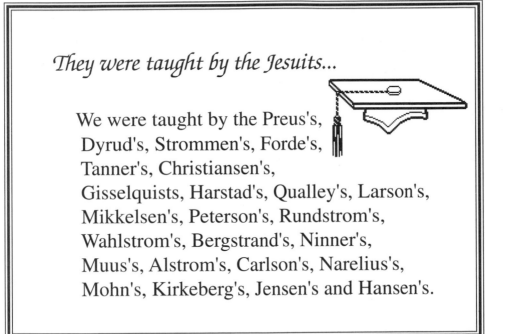

They were taught by the Jesuits...

We were taught by the Preus's, Dyrud's, Strommen's, Forde's, Tanner's, Christiansen's, Gisselquists, Harstad's, Qualley's, Larson's, Mikkelsen's, Peterson's, Rundstrom's, Wahlstrom's, Bergstrand's, Ninner's, Muus's, Alstrom's, Carlson's, Narelius's, Mohn's, Kirkeberg's, Jensen's and Hansen's.

They found enrichment at Notre Dame and Creighton University...
We found it at *Norskedalen, Skogfjorden* and *Vesterheim.*

They avoided the draft by attending Loyala...
We avoided the draft by going to Luther Sem.

They gave up chocolate for Lent...
We gave it up for skin reasons.

They called us heathens, sinners, and publics...
   We called them minnow-munchers,
   mackerel-snappers, and toe-kissers.

They lived in Reynolds, ND and Brandon,
MN...
   We lived in Buxton, ND and
   Evansville, MN.

They had 240 first cousins...
   We had 20 to 70.

They sprinkled Holy Water...
    We sprinkled lefse and the ironing.

They had leprechauns...
    We had *nisser.*

They had Midnight Mass on Christmas Eve...
    We had Sunday School Christmas Programs.

They had Pat and Mike...
    We had: Ole and Lena,
            Toivo and Eino,
            Slim and Spud,
            Ola and Per.

They debated the encyclical letters...
    We debated the work of the various hymnal
    committees.

They had Irish and Italian relatives...
    We had Swedish and Danish relatives.

They had German relatives...
    We had German relatives.

They knew German-Catholics...
    We knew German-Lutherans.

They had the Benedictines...
   We had the Benson's.

They were named the McCoy's...
   We were named the Melgaard's.

They were called Pascuali...
   We were called Peterson.

They had names that began with O or Mac and ended with ...elli, ...ich, or ...ani...

We had names that began with men's first names and ended in ...son or ...sen or in ...sson or ...ssen.

They have Karol Wojtyla...*

We have King Oscar.

....

*Pope John Paul II

They had eternal flames...
We had pilot lights.

They had Mary, Joseph, Theresa, Francis, Rose and Patrick...
We had Marta, Hjalmar, Ingeborg, Trygve, Johan and Nettie.

They prayed that their kids would become priests or nuns...
We prayed that our kids would *turn out.*

Music

They had the Sistine Choir...
We had the St. Olaf Choir.

They had the Vienna Boys' Choir...
We had the Nordkapp Male Chorus.

They had the Singing Nuns...
We had women's triple trios.

They had Mozart's Mass in C Minor...
We had John Thompson, Book Three.

They sang Gregorian chants...
We sang *"Jesus Loves Me"*.

They had the Living Rosary,
(50 girls with boys interspersed for the "Glory Be's") ...
We had antiphonal and choral readings.

They had altar boys...
   We had the junior choir.

They sang "St. Therese of the Roses"...
   We sang *"In the Garden"*.

They had Pope Gregor, the Chanter...
   We had John Ylvisaker.

They had Scarlatti and Saint-Saëns ...
We had Grieg and Grundtvig.

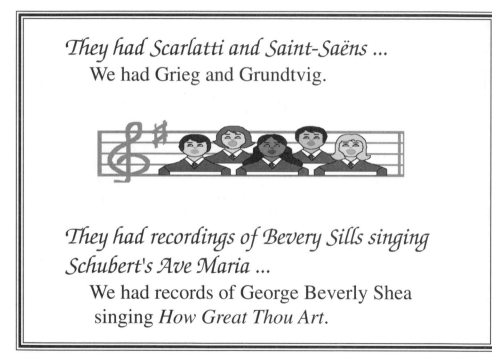

They had recordings of Bevery Sills singing Schubert's Ave Maria ...
We had records of George Beverly Shea singing *How Great Thou Art*.

*They had Antonio Salieri and
Antonio Stradivari...*
> We had Jan Sibelius and Ole Bull.

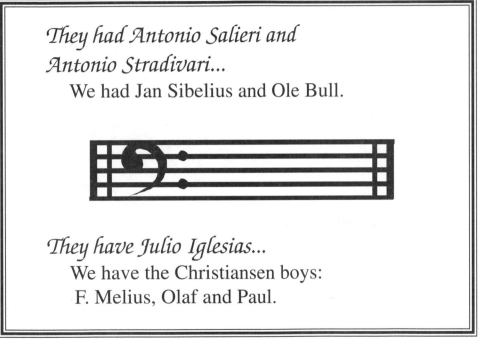

They have Julio Iglesias...
> We have the Christiansen boys:
> F. Melius, Olaf and Paul.

On one hand...

They had oratorios...
 and we had cantatas,

and

They sang "Ave Maria"...
 and we sang "Away in the Manger",

but, this was in cathedrals.

On the other hand...

They had thin song books...
and we had thick hymnals,

and while

They sang the melody line...
We learned and sang all four parts.

Of course, this was at the local level.

They read the Catholic Digest...
　　We read the **Lutheran Standard**.

They have the Vatican Press...
　　We have Augsburg Publishing
　　House.

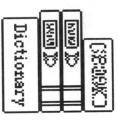

They got their medieval fixes by reading the Canterbury Tales...
　　We got ours reading **Kristin Lavransdatter**.

They had the Basilica of St. Mary's on Hennepin...

We had the Swedish Institute
on Park.

They had the Vatican...

We had Vesterheim.

They had Rodin's sculptures...
  We had butter sculptures.

They had gargoyles on their churches...
  We had dragon heads on ours.

They had Michelangelo...
    We had Edvard Munch.

They had Michelangelo's "David"...
    We had Eric Enstrom's *"Grace"*.

They had the Sistine Chapel...
We had Heddal *Stavkirke*.

They had stained glass...
We had stained tablecloths.

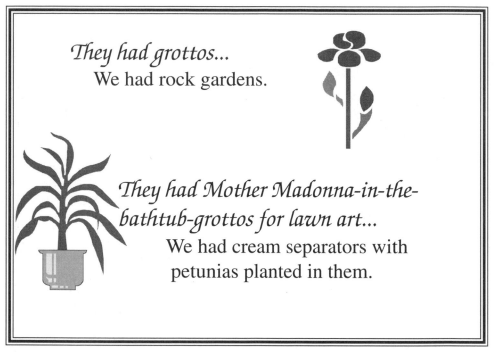

They had grottos...
We had rock gardens.

They had Mother Madonna-in-the-bathtub-grottos for lawn art...
We had cream separators with petunias planted in them.

Chapter X

LOW BROW STUFF:
Fellowship and Recreation

They had a May procession...
We had *barnetoget* May 17.

They celebrated March 17...
We celebrated May 17.

They had Mary May Day...
We had *syttende mai.*

They went to church carnivals...
   We went to Sunday School picnics.

They went to Rosary Club...
   We went to Ladies Aid with lunch.

They hosted Sodolity Club...
   We hosted circles.

They worked their way around the Rosary...
We played *Ring Around the Rosey.*

They had fish on the calendar to mark Days of Abstinence...
We had it to mark the opening of fishing season.

They had Cardinal Spellman...
We had Per Spelmann.

They were the Fightin' Irish...
   We were the Vikings.

They belonged to bowling leagues...
   We belonged to Luther League.

They played pool...
   We played shuffleboard.

They cheered for Jean-Claude Killy...
  We cheered for Ingemar Johanssen.

They belonged to the Knights of Columbus...
  We belonged to Sons of Norway.

They went to bullfights in Spain...
  We had the Battle of Stikklestad.

They drove big Buick station wagons...
    We drove Chevy or Ford sedans.

They hung out on John Ireland Boulevard...
    We hung out on Snoose / *snus* Boulevard.

They were often celibate...
    We were too, even if we were happily
    married.

Chapter XI

PLACES TO GO:
Meccas, Pilgrimages,
Schools, Cities, etc.

They took pilgrimages to Medjugorje...
    We took tours of the Holy Land.

They went to Villa Maria...
    We went to Holden Village.

They went to Fatima...
    We went to Rapid City.

They had Rome...
   We had Augsburg.

They had the Vatican...
   We had Trondheim.

They had St. Peter's Square...
   We had *Nidarosdomen.*

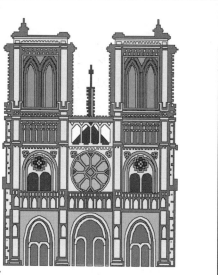

They had shrines...
We had gardens.

They had shrines...
Our homes were our castles.

They went to Lourdes to get healed...
We went to the doctor.

For pilgrimages,

They went to Banneux, Belgium...
We went to the *Høstfest.*

They went to Beauvaign, Belgium...
We went to the Nordic Fest.

They went to La Salette, France...
We went to *Svenskarnasdag.*

They went to Knock, Ireland...
 We went to the *Hjemkomst* Festival.

They went to Guadalupe, Mexico...
 We went to Norway Day in Minnehaha
 Park.

They went to Catalina Island...
 We went to the Lofoten Islands.

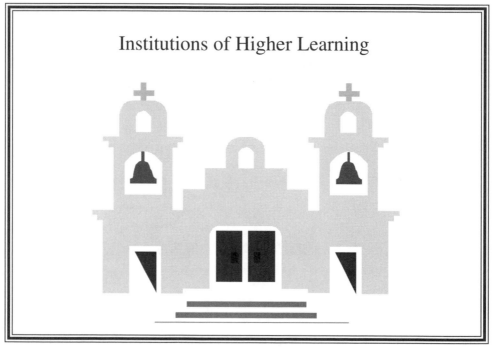

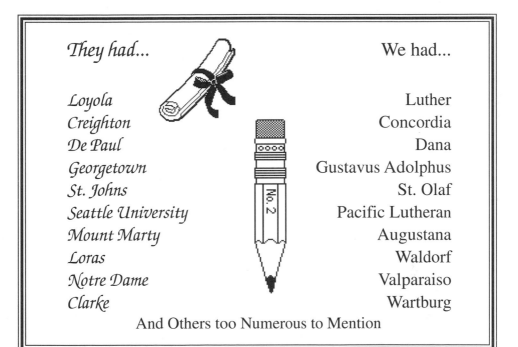

They had...

We had...

Loyola	Luther
Creighton	Concordia
De Paul	Dana
Georgetown	Gustavus Adolphus
St. Johns	St. Olaf
Seattle University	Pacific Lutheran
Mount Marty	Augustana
Loras	Waldorf
Notre Dame	Valparaiso
Clarke	Wartburg

And Others too Numerous to Mention

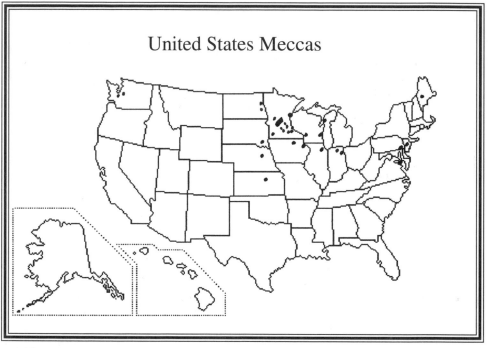

They went to...

Baltimore, MD
Boston, MA
Dubuque, IA
Milwaukee, WI
New Prague, MN
St. Cloud, MN
South Bend, IN
Washington, D.C.
St. Paul, MN

We went to...

Ballard, WA
Blair, NE
Decorah, IA
Muskego, WI
Northfield, MN
St. Croix Falls, MN
Sioux Falls, SD
Washington Island, WI
Minneapolis, MN

They had...

STEARNS COUNTY

We had..

Poulsbo, WA	Westby, WI
Tyler, MN	Askov, MN
Elkhart, IN	New Sweden, ME
Lindsborg, KA	Scandia, MN
Fox River, IL	Bishop Hill, IL

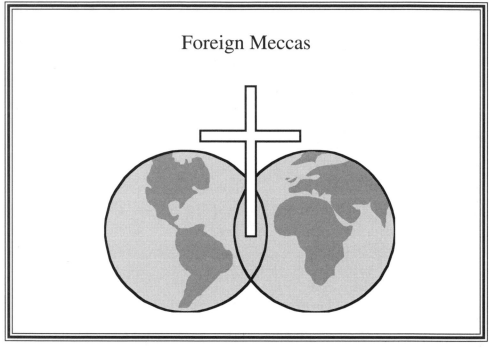

Foreign Meccas

They went to...	We went to...
Belfast	Belfast
Barcelona	Bergen
Cordoba	Copenhagen (Köbenhavn)
Dublin	Dalarna
Florence	Flensburg
Genoa	Göteborg
Guadalajara	Grimstad
Honduras	Helsinki
Lisbon	Lillehammer
Madrid	Malmö
Mexico City	Molde
Milan	Mora
Naples	Nord Trøndelag
Ostrava	Oslo
Paris	Porsgrunn
Rome	Reykjavik
Seville	Stavanger
Sicily	Stockholm
Venice	Värmland

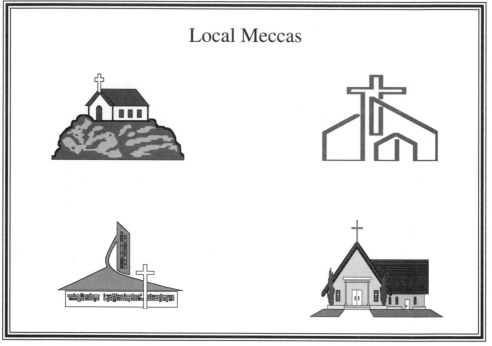

Local Meccas

They went to...   We went to...

They went to...	We went to...
Our Lady of Lourde's	Augustana Lutheran
St. Bridget's	Faith Lutheran
St. Anne's	Central Lutheran
Immaculate Conception	Immanuel Lutheran
St. Francis Xavier	Our Saviour's Lutheran
Our Lady of Fatima	Bethlehem Lutheran
St. Peter's	Mt. Olivet Lutheran
Holy Name	Hosanna Lutheran
Holy Cross	Calvary Lutheran
Holy Martyr's	Zion Lutheran
St. Mary's	First Lutheran

After they turned,.	After we *turned,*
they went to...	<u>we</u> went to...

Christ Lutheran	*Our Lady of Mt. Carmel*
Hope Lutheran	*St. Francis of Assisi*
Peace Lutheran	*Annunciation*
Trinity Lutheran	*Assumption*
Elim Lutheran	*St. Theresa's*
Our Redeemer's Lutheran	*St. Michael's*
Our Saviour's Lutheran	*St. Joseph's*
Bethany Lutheran	*St. Pious, the X*
Bethel Lutheran	*Our Lady of the Blessed Sacrament*
St. Olaf Lutheran	*St. Cecelia's*
Prince of Peace Lutheran	*Pax Christi*

Chapter XII

DEAD ENDS
and
THE END

They had the Last Rites...
    We had pastoral visitation and
    the Sunshine Club volunteers.

They patronized O'Malley's Mortuary...
    We went to Peterson's Funeral Parlor.

They had Faure's "Requiem"...
    We had *"Den Store Hvite Flok"*.

They had wakes where everybody came, hugged, and bawled...

We had visitations and went there when we hoped no family would be there, signed the book, and left to hurry home to make the family a *Hotdish* to bring to the house, and a cake for the church basement funeral lunch the next day.

Their mourners came to grieve and console...
   Ours came to pay their respects,
   be seen, and have lunch.

Their departed loved ones looked kind of puffy...
   Ours looked kind of *peaked*.

They were buried with their Rosaries...
   We were buried in our funeral suits.

They had purgatory and limbo options...
  We had no in-between.

Their cemeteries had statues of Mary and the Saints...
  Ours had geraniums and weeping willows.

They had plots for ten to twelve...
  We had plots for two or four.

They had tombstones...
    We had gravemarkers.

Their tombstones read,
"*Gratias Agamus Domino Deo Nostro*"...*

    Ours read, "*Takk for Alt*".**

....
  *Let us give Thanks to the Lord
**Thanks for Everything

They had ejaculations...
>   We're done explaining their behavior.
>   No more needs to be said.

Their last utterance was the ejaculation,
"Jesus, Mary, and Joseph"...
>   Ours was, "*Uffda, Neimen du, da*"!

THE END

ORDER FORM for <u>They Glorified Mary...</u>
(A Catholic-Lutheran Lexicon)

Name_____

Address_____

City_____St_____Zip_____

No. of Copies_____ @ $6.95   **Subtotal**:$_____
        (Canada $8.95)

Plus Postage & handling (per book)
    1st Class $2.00 per book $_____
    Book Rate $1.50 per book $_____
(Maximum postage cost for multiple orders: $6.00)
    MN Residents add 6.5 % Sales Tax $_____
                          TOTAL:$_____

Send cash, check or money order to: Caragana Press
                                   Box 396
                                   Hastings, MN 55033

ORDER FORM for <u>Cream Peas on Toast</u>

Name_____

Address _____

City_____St_____Zip_____

No. of Copies_____ @ $9.95   **Subtotal**: $_____

Plus Postage & handling (per book)

    1st Class $3.00 per book $_____

    Book Rate $1.50 per book $_____

(Maximum postage cost for multiple orders: $6.00)

    MN Residents add 6.5 % Sales Tax $_____

                          TOTAL:$_____

Send cash, check or money order to: Caragana Press

                                       Box 396

                                       Hastings, MN 55033

ORDER FORM for <u>They Had Stores...</u>
(A Town-Country Lexicon)

Name_____

Address _____

City_____St_____Zip_____

No. of Copies_____ @ $6.95   **Subtotal**: $_____
          (Canada $8.95)

Plus Postage & handling (per book)

   1st Class $2.00 per book $_____

   Book Rate $1.50 per book $_____

(Maximum postage cost for multiple orders: $6.00)

   MN Residents add 6.5 % Sales Tax $ _____

                              TOTAL: $_____

Send cash, check or money order to: Caragana Press

                                      Box 396

                                      Hastings, MN 55033